# Do It Yourself Projects!

# Make Your Own Musical Instruments

# Anna-Marie D'Cruz

PowerKiDS press

New York

Published in 2009 by The Rosen Publishing Group Inc.
29 East 21st Street, New York, NY 10010

First Edition

Senior Editor: Jennifer Schofield
Designer: Jason Billin
Project maker: Anna-Marie D'Cruz
Photographer: Chris Fairclough
Proofreader: Susie Brooks

Library of Congress Cataloging-in-Publication Data

D'Cruz, Anna-Marie.
  Make your own musical instruments / Anna-Marie D'Cruz. — 1st ed.
      p. cm. — (Do it yourself projects!)
  Includes index.
  ISBN 978-1-4358-2854-4 (library binding)
  ISBN 978-1-4358-2925-1 (paperback)
  ISBN 978-1-4358-2926-8 (6-pack)
  1. Musical instruments—Construction—Juvenile literature. I. Title.
  ML460.D37 2009
  784.192'3—dc22

                                    2008033667

Manufactured in China

Acknowledgments
The Publisher would like to thank the following models:
Emel Augustin, Jade Campbell, Ammar Duffus, Akash Kohli,
Ellie Lawrence, Adam Menditta, Eloise Ramplin, Robin Stevens.

Picture Credits:
Alll photography by Chris Fairclough except for
pages 2, 4, 8 bottom left Hachette Children's books; page 5 top
Lindsay Hebberd/CORBIS; page 7 bottom right Pete aloutos/CORBIS

### Note to parents and teachers:
The projects in this book are designed
to be made by children. However, we
recommend adult supervision at all times
since the Publisher cannot be held
responsible for any injury caused while
making the projects.

# Contents

# All about musical instruments

People have used musical instruments for thousands of years to make tuneful and rhythmic sounds. They are played in many different ways all over the world.

## TYPES OF INSTRUMENTS

There are four different groups of musical instrument: percussion, string, wind, and keyboard.

Percussion instruments, such as drums and cymbals, can be hit, clashed together, shaken, or even scraped to produce a sound.

String instruments (see left), such as the violin and harp, give out a sound from their strings when played with a bow or plucked with the fingers. The strings are stretched over a hollow wooden box, which makes the sound louder.

Wind instruments, including the flute and trumpet (see below), are tubes made from wood or metal that the player blows into. This is sometimes through a reed, or by vibrating the lips, like blowing a raspberry, into a mouthpiece.

Keyboard instruments, such as the piano and synthesizer, use sets of keys, levers, and buttons, which are pressed down to hammer out a note.

# CULTURE AND MUSIC

Music plays an important role in many cultures and religions. For example, Spanish dancers use instruments known as castanets when they dance the flamenco. In Africa, ankle rattles, sometimes made from insect cocoons with seeds or stones inside them, are worn during tribal dances (see left). Dancers shake the rattles to add rhythm.

Tribesmen of the rain forests in South America dance with an instrument called the rainmaker, made from the hollow stems of dried cactus plants. They rattle it to call on the gods to bring rain. In the Bhuddist religion, bells and drums give ceremonies a rythmic beat.

## GET STARTED!

In this book, you can discover ways of making interesting musical instruments from around the world. Try to use materials that you already have, either at home or at school. For example, for the cardboard in these projects, the backs of used-up notepads, writing pads, art pads, and hardbacked envelopes are ideal. Reusing and recyling materials like this is good for the environment and it will save you money. The projects have all been made and decorated for this book, but do not worry if yours look a little different—just have fun making and playing your instruments.

# Spanish castanets

Castanets are percussion instruments that are held in the hand. They are used in flamenco dancing to tap out a rhythm. Can you click your own rhythm with these fun castanets?

## YOU WILL NEED

piece of colored card,
   6 x 3 in. (15 x 8cm)

2 buttons 1½ in. (4cm) wide

pencil

pair of scissors

colored paper

glue

20 in. (50cm) cord

masking tape

adhesive pads

**1** Fold the card in half. Put a button in the center of one side of the card. Draw the shape shown around it, making sure the circular part is wider than the button. With the card still folded, cut out the shape but do not cut along the fold.

folded edge

**2** Cut out shapes from the colored paper and glue them to the outside of the castanets.

**3** Tie a double knot at each end of the cord. Stick the middle of the cord to the inside of the fold with masking tape.

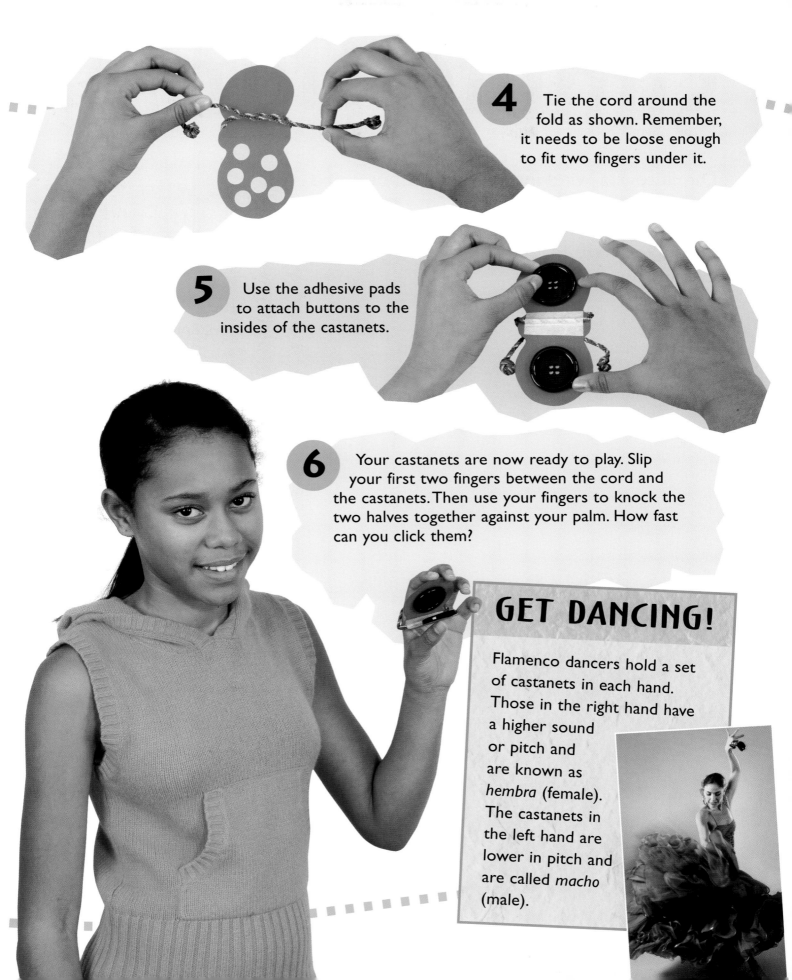

**4** Tie the cord around the fold as shown. Remember, it needs to be loose enough to fit two fingers under it.

**5** Use the adhesive pads to attach buttons to the insides of the castanets.

**6** Your castanets are now ready to play. Slip your first two fingers between the cord and the castanets. Then use your fingers to knock the two halves together against your palm. How fast can you click them?

## GET DANCING!

Flamenco dancers hold a set of castanets in each hand. Those in the right hand have a higher sound or pitch and are known as *hembra* (female). The castanets in the left hand are lower in pitch and are called *macho* (male).

# Simple flute

The flute is a wind instrument, so notes are made by blowing into it. This flute is easy to make and does not need many materials. When you have made it, try blowing your favorite tunes.

**YOU WILL NEED**

4 strips of paper, each
1¼ x 3¼ in. (3 x 8cm)
masking tape
2 clean long popsicle sticks
waxed paper
colored tape

**1** Fold each strip of paper in half lengthwise three times to make a small block.

**2** Tape two blocks of paper the same distance in from each end of one of the popsicle sticks. Now do the same for the other stick.

## WIND POWER

The first wind instruments were made from animal bones with holes down the side, a little like today's recorders. Since then, wind instruments have been made from wood and metal.

**3** Cut a rectangle of waxed paper that is twice the width of the sticks and long enough to cover the paper blocks. Fold it in half along the longest piece.

**4** Place a popsicle stick in front of you with the paper blocks facing upward. Lay the strip of waxed paper on top of the stick and tape it to the ends of the stick. Make sure the waxed paper is as straight and as tight as possible.

**5** Lay the second popsicle stick on top of the other stick with the paper blocks facing downward. Wrap some tape around both popsicle sticks to hold everything together.

**6** Blow through the sticks with the folded edge of waxed paper toward you. This makes the surfaces of the waxed paper vibrate, producing a noise. If you gently squeeze the sticks together as you blow, you can change the pitch of the note.

# Bongo drums

Bongo drums are believed to have come from Cuba and are traditionally made from two different-sized drums. Make these colorful bongos and beat your favorite song.

## YOU WILL NEED

plastic shopping bag

pair of scissors

2 empty potato chip tubes with no lids, different sizes

permanent marker

masking tape

colored paper

glue

2 strips of stiff cardboard ¾ in. (2cm) wide and 1½ in. (4cm) longer than the shorter tube

ruler

paint and paintbrush

double-sided tape

**1** Cut down one side and across the bottom of the shopping bag, so that you have a single layer of plastic. Put a tube on the plastic and draw around it. Cut out the circle, adding an extra 2 in. (5cm) all around. Do the same for the second tube.

**2** Place a circle of plastic over the open end of a tube. Using pieces of masking tape, stick the plastic down all around the side. Keep pulling the plastic tightly as you do this. Wrap another piece of tape around the tube to make sure the plastic is stuck firmly. Do the same with the second tube.

## MAKE SOME NOISE!

The drums are different sizes so that they make different sounds. The sound a drum makes also depends on its shape, what it is made from, and how tight the skin at the top of the drum is.

**3** Cut a sheet of colored paper large enough to go around each tube. Decorate it with different shapes and colors of paper. Wrap the decorated sheets around the tubes and glue them down.

**4** Tape the two strips of cardboard together, end to end with each strip overlapping the other by 1½ in. (4cm).

**5** Fold up each side of the overlap and put tape around the ends of the strips to form a triangle. Decorate the triangle by painting it. Stick the triangle to the tubes with double-sided tape, making sure the base of the triangle is at the top of the tubes.

**6** To play the bongos, put them between your knees and gently tap the tops with your fingertips. Can you hear a different sound from each drum?

# Jazz washboard

Washboards were originally used for washing clothes. People doing their laundry noticed that the corrugated surface made a good sound when they scraped their fingers over it. Make a washboard and create some jazz!

**1** Draw a line across the stiff card 1¼ in. (3cm) from the top. Then draw lines down the card, 1¼ in. (3cm) in from each side. Draw a line across the card 4 in. (10cm) from the bottom.

**2** Draw another line 2¾ in. (7cm) from the bottom of the card and cut around it, making sure you are left with the shape shown.

## SPOONS, KAZOOS, AND JUGS

Washboards are played by musicians in a jug band. Members of a jug band play instruments made from things found in the home, such as a jug, spoons, and a kazoo. A *kazoo* is a comb covered in tissue paper that is blown across to make a tune. What other things from around your house could you use to make music?

**3** Glue down the corrugated paper in the center of your frame, making sure that the grooves go across the frame.

**4** Cover your work surface with newspaper. Use paint to decorate the strips of corrugated cardboard and allow them to dry.

**5** When the paint has dried, glue the two long strips of corrugated cardboard, one to each side of the washboard. Then glue the two short strips across the top and bottom. When the glue has dried, the washboard is ready to play.

**6** Use a pencil to scrape up and down the washboard. Experiment with short and long scrapes to see what sort of tune you can make.

# African thumb piano

Thumb pianos are played by plucking keys. The keys are fixed to a wooden box or a hollowed gourd. Follow these steps to make a thumb piano and create a gentle melody.

**1** Place one of the card squares down on your work surface. Arrange five of the stirrers so that they match those in the picture.

**2** Glue the first stirrer down in place. Glue the next stirrer ⅝ in. (1.5cm) farther out over the end of the card. Glue down the remaining stirrers, moving each one out another ⅝ in. (1.5cm) farther than the previous one.

**3** Measure six 4 in. (10cm) strips from the extra card, wide enough to fit the gaps between the stirrers. Cut them out and glue them to the card between the stirrers.

**4** Glue the other square of card over the top to cover the stirrers up and allow to dry.

# GOOD VIBRATIONS

Any sound we hear is a result of something moving. With the thumb piano, the quivering movement, known as vibration, of the plucked sticks makes the sound. Vibrations are made louder, or amplified, with the use of a hollow container, known as a sound box.

**5** Cover your work surface with newspaper. Paint the square. With the end of the spare wooden stirrer, scratch a design into the square. Allow the square to dry. Then paint alternate keys black.

**6** When all the paint has dried, place the piano on top of the shoe box, which will act as a sound box. Hold down the piano with one hand while you twang the keys with your fingers on the other. Experiment on different surfaces to see if you can create different sounds.

# Hand drum

The chod drum is a small, double-sided hand drum. It is used by Buddhist monks during meditation. To play the drum, you need to twist your hand so that the knots swing from side to side, hitting the drumheads.

## YOU WILL NEED

- 2 shoelaces, about 14 in. (35cm) long
- empty cardboard circular cheese tub
- stapler
- masking tape
- paint and paintbrush
- pair of scissors
- colored card
- glue
- double-sided tape
- 40 in. (1m) of wide ribbon

**1** Staple one end of each shoelace to the inside of the bottom of the tub. The laces need to be directly opposite each other. Stick a piece of tape over each staple.

**2** Cut each lace so that it reaches beyond the middle of the side of the drum. Make a knot at the end of each shoelace.

**3** Put the lid back on the tub with the laces hanging on the outside of it. Tape the tub shut all the way around, taping over the laces.

**4** Paint the rims of the tub and allow them to dry. Add a strip of colored card around the side of the tub.

**5** Cut circles of card big enough to cover the lid and bottom of the tub. Glue the card down and decorate it with shapes of colored card.

**6** Stick double-sided tape around the edge of the tub. Place the tub on your work surface, with the lid facing upward and the laces on the left and right.

**7** Glue down the center of the piece of ribbon at the far side of the tub edge. Then stick the ribbon around the edge. Staple the ribbon together where the ends meet at the bottom.

**8** The hand drum is now ready to play. Hold onto the ribbon, and place your fingertips at the bottom of the drum. Twist your wrist and watch the laces swing from side to side.

## CHANTING MONKS

Buddhists are people who follow the religious beliefs of a man called Siddharta Gautama. Buddhist monks are men who give up their possessions and family to spend time studying holy books, chanting, and meditating.

# Shaking maracas

Maracas are popular in Latin America. They were originally made from hollowed-out gourds that had been left to dry. The steps below make one maraca, so you will need to repeat the instructions to make another one.

## YOU WILL NEED

For each maraca:

newspaper

small balloon

small beaker

craft glue mixed with water (see box on page 19)

small pieces of white paper

pair of scissors

funnel

2 tablespoons of dry rice

thin card

small stapler

masking tape

paints and paintbrush

**1** Begin by laying out sheets of newspaper over your work area. Blow up a balloon to the size you would like your maraca to be and knot it. Rest it on a beaker with the knotted part facing upward.

**2** To papier mâché the balloon, stick pieces of newspaper with lots of the glue and water mixture on the balloon. Leave a space around the knot. When you have built four layers over the balloon, go over it with a layer of white paper. Allow the balloon to dry.

**3** When the balloon is dry, hold onto the knot and carefully pop the balloon with a pair of scissors. Remove any pieces of balloon stuck in the paper shell. Rest the shell on the beaker with the hole at the top. Use the funnel to pour the rice in.

**4** To make a handle for the maraca, roll up the thin card into a tube. It must be big enough to sit over the hole of the ball and long enough for you to hold.

**5** Put the handle together using a stapler. Then snip a short way up around one end of the tube. Fan the snipped pieces out. Sit the fanned end over the hole in the ball and stick it down with pieces of tape. Tape up the other end of the handle.

**6** Papier mâché the handle with a few layers of white paper.

**7** While the handle is drying, make the second maraca by repeating steps one to six. When both are completely dry, paint the maracas with bright-colored patterns. When the paint is dry, dance and shake your maracas.

## GET CRAFTY!

Papier mâché is a way of creating shapes from a paper and glue mixture, which dry hard and can then be painted. Your mixture of glue and water should be more runny than glue, but not watery. Try adding the water a teaspoon at a time, to make sure you do not add too much water.

# Egyptian harp

Harps were played in Ancient Egypt. They came in many different shapes and sizes. Some had only a few strings, but others had more than 20. This Egyptian harp takes time to make, but it is worth the effort!

## YOU WILL NEED

small shoe box

pair of scissors

wooden coat hanger with removable hook

pencil

4 paper fasteners

very strong tape

colored card

paint and paintbrush

double-sided tape

4 long rubber bands

**1** Take the lid off the shoe box. Cut a slit just over halfway down the middle of one end of the box, as wide as the edge of the hanger.

**2** Mark four points down the middle of the top of the lid. Push through a paper fastener at each point, and open it up on the underside. Put the lid back on the box and tape around it to seal the box. Do not tape over the slit.

**3** Using the picture as a guide, draw an animal's head on the colored card. Draw the neck slightly longer so that you can tape it to the box. Cut out the head and decorate it. Decorate the rest of the box.

## EGYPTIANS AND MUMMIES

Animals were very important to the Ancient Egyptians. They believed that some animals had supernatural powers. Often, when the animals died, they were mummified, so that they could be buried with their owners.

**4** Make a ½ in. (1cm) slit at the bottom of the head to make tabs. Bend tabs in opposite directions. Tape the head to the end of the box without the slit with double-sided tape.

**5** Ask an adult to help you to remove the hook from the coat hanger. Using strong tape, stick a rubber band to the center of the hanger. Tape three more rubber bands as shown.

**6** Ask an adult to help you with this step. Push the end of the hanger without the rubber bands into the slit at the back of the box. Rest it on the bottom of the box. While holding the hanger up, stretch the lowest rubber band to hook it onto nearest fastener. Repeat with the other rubber bands, each time moving up the hanger and hooking onto the next fastener.

**7** The harp is now ready to play. Either rest it on a table or place it between your knees and pluck the rubber bands. Can you play a gentle tune?

# Glossary

**amplify**

To amplify sounds is to make them stronger or louder. On a thumb piano, the soundbox amplifies the sound.

**Buddhists**

People who follow the teachings or religious beliefs of Siddharta Gautama.

**chanting**

Saying or calling words out in a special rhythm. Some religions, such as Buddhism, use chanting as a way to pray.

**drumheads**

The part of the drum that you beat against, often with your hand or a stick.

**flamenco**

A type of dance done mainly in Spain. Flamenco dancers use castanets to tap out the rhythmn of their dance.

**gourd**

The hard skin of a fruit. The skin is hollowed out and dried to make musical instruments.

**keyboard instruments**

Musical instruments that have levers, pedals, and keys that are pushed or pressed to create a note. Pianos and organs are keyboard instruments.

**Latin America**

Parts of Central and South America where Spanish and Portuguese are the main languages spoken.

**meditating**

To meditate is to think deeply and seriously about something. Some religions use meditation as a type of prayer.

**monks**

Holy men that live in monasteries.

**mummify**

To treat a body with oils and wrap it in cloth to preserve it after it has been burried.

**papier mâché**

Paper that has been made into a pulp or layered with a glue and water mixture to make objects that are solid when they dry.

## percussion instruments

Musical instruments that are shaken, beaten, hit together, or scraped to make a sound. Drums are a type of percussion instrument.

## pitch

How low or high a voice or musical note sounds. Men usually have low-pitched voices and women have high-pitched voices.

## recycling

To recycle something is to change it or treat it so that it can be used again.

## sound box

The hollow part of a stringed instrument that amplifies the sound, making it louder or stronger.

## string instruments

Musical instruments that have strings that need to be plucked, pulled, or combed to make a sound. Guitars, harps, and cellos are all string instruments.

## vibrations

Vibrations happen when something moves to and fro very quickly. This makes a quivering sound.

## wind instruments

Musical instruments that are blown or sucked to make a sound. Flutes and recorders are wind instruments.

# FURTHER INFORMATION

## BOOKS TO READ

**Make a Joyful Noisemaker**
by Mark Burrows
(Abingdon Press, 2006)

**Making Music**
by Ann Sayre Wiseman and John Langstaff
(Storey Publishing, 2003)

## WEB SITES

Due to the changing nature of Internet links, PowerKids Press has developed an online list of Web sites related to the subject of this book. This site is updated regularly. Please use this link to access this list:
www.powerkidslinks.com/diyp/musical

# Index